CW00500541

(10 WAYS TO)
BUILD YOUR
SELF-CONFIDENCE

BY AMANDA CRAVEN

Amanda Craven MSc(Psychol), Dip Hyp, Cert Life Coach
www.notjustcoaching.com

For Anne and Joe, my treasured parents, with all my love

INTRODUCTION

Welcome to my latest 'no-fluff' guide!

Here, I'm sharing some easy to practise exercises that will help you flex your self-confidence muscles. There is a slight progression as you work through the short chapters but you can just as easily dip in to whatever you feel you need first.

For the purpose of simplicity I have mostly used the term self-confidence although the exercises are suitable for working on both self-esteem, self-worth **and** self-confidence. There are differences between the terms, but I want this to be a practical, hit-the-ground-running type of guide and don't think it's the place to start trawling through definitions. **You** know what you struggle with, and what you need most help with - and that's all that matters!

I share a few little case studies in this book but have used different names and changed minor details to avoid any possible identification. Sometimes telling a story is simply the best way to get a message across.

This book is intended to be a tool for you to use as and when it suits you. Having said that, I always encourage readers and clients to take regular baby steps and 'chip away' at changes they want to make.

So dive in, take those baby steps, and know that YOU HAVE GOT THIS!

Amanda

PS See the end of the book for ways to keep in touch.

1. THIS IS ME!

Self-confidence and healthy self-esteem begin with self-acceptance. Self-acceptance cannot happen if we don't even know who we really are.

Each one of us is unique. It is okay to be unique and to like/dislike different things to others.

When you were a child you had to conform to the expectations of others in so many ways. Now you're an adult you can choose how to live your life. You can make choices that are aligned with YOUR values, beliefs and goals. If you never had the chance to develop those things this exercise is a great place to start.

Write notes in all the following sections to remind yourself who you are. Remember there are no wrong answers. Write the first things that come to mind - you can always add other thoughts later.

Exercise 1 - This is Me

I like doing/eating/listening to/being in...

I don't like...

I feel safe/comfortable when...

I don't feel safe/comfortable when...

I'm scared of...

I'm not scared of...

I feel calm/peaceful when...

I feel agitated/anxious when...

I want to...

I don't want to...

I'd like more...

I'd like less...

I'd like to do more…(even if I'm not sure I could)

I'd like to do less…(even if I don't think it's possible)

I like the following about myself…

I don't like the following about myself…

I'd like to …

I need...

I don't need...

THIS IS WHO I AM AND I ACCEPT THAT I AM
PERFECTLY ME.

THERE MAY BE SOME THINGS THAT I WANT TO
CHANGE TO MAKE MY LIFE BETTER. AND THAT'S
OKAY, TOO.

I WILL UNDERTAKE ANY CHANGES WITH PATIENCE,
KINDNESS AND TAKE BABY STEPS.

SIGNED:

DATE:

2. A PROMISE TO YOUR INNER CHILD

We come into this world without an ounce of self-consciousness, trusting that all our needs will be met and that we will be loved unconditionally. We don't question our worth or worthiness.

It is therefore the people around us as we grow who either reinforce our worthiness, loveability and belonging or teach us (through actions and/or words) that we are not acceptable or lovable and we do not belong.

These people may be parents, carers, other family members, teachers, neighbours and other children. Later in life they may be a partner, colleague or friend.

Researchers believe that the way we are treated in the first three months of life has the biggest impact on our sense of self-worth as an adult. If we weren't shown unconditional love and if our needs weren't met in those first few weeks of life it is more difficult (though not at all impossible) to learn to regulate our self-esteem as an adult*.

This exercise will help you reconnect with your younger self and re-write those (now unhelpful and defunct) 'rules for life' that you lived by in the past.

Exercise 2 - Make a Promise to Your Inner Child

1. Find photos of your younger self (from any age but include some from as far back as possible).

2. Put them in front of you and let yourself be drawn to one (or do 'eeny meeny miny mo'!)

3. Look at the picture for a few minutes, noticing what comes up and see what you can remember about life at that time.

4. Close your eyes and either remember – or imagine (if you haven't got memories of that time) – some of the tricky things going on in the life of your younger self. Using the wisdom and knowledge you have now, reassure them that everything that happens will make them grow into someone special and unique – even the tricky stuff* will teach them about life AND will stop. They won't have to struggle forever because they will grow up into an adult who is in charge of themselves, who can make their own decisions and choices.

5. Look into the eyes of that beautiful little person and begin telling them what a wonderful human being they are. Tell them that you are going to take care of them, love them unconditionally, support them and help them grow and live the life they deserve to live.

6. Now it's time to remind them that they have got all the tools inside them that they will need to deal with whatever life brings to their door. Ask them to lift up their head, stand tall, and SMILE. Tell them all the things you know they will learn, and that they will find their own way to do what feels right for them. You can say these words out loud or write them as a letter to your younger self. Either way you may use the 'script' below to give you some ideas.

You can repeat the exercise as many times (and for as many photos) as you like!

This exercise may be very emotional for you. Take a break if you need to. If you suffered abuse or neglect of any kind (or if you believe you may have done) please work through *these issues with a professional therapist and <u>don't try to do this alone</u>.*

It's great to use your own words but you can use this little script as inspiration for your conversation/letter:

"Hello! I'm grown up [Amanda].

I can see that you're [at school] in this picture and live in [Lancashire] with your 2 little sisters and Mum and Dad. You play out on the street with your friend Fiona. Your car often breaks down on the way to school and you get told off for being late a lot.

I know some things can feel a bit tricky at the moment, and life/people can be confusing. Sometimes you get told off at school and at home for things you don't understand. Sometimes it's okay to make up your mind what you're going to do and grown ups find you funny, but other times they seem to get angry for no reason. This happens because grown ups are usually very busy and make assumptions and quick judgements that are not always the right ones.

One day YOU will be a busy grown up, but YOU will remember to stop and try to understand why children and young people do things before getting annoyed or shouting. This is just one way that you will use all your experiences from this time to become an excellent adult.

I also know that you often feel a bit different to other children at school, and you don't feel you belong like they do. In actual fact, most people (big and small) feel this way but become very good at hiding it or pretending they are okay. Maybe you do think differently to others sometimes, but this is a special gift that makes you unique and it will help you to do certain jobs better than some people when you're a grown up.

When you're an adult you will be the one making decisions and will be able to choose where you want to live and who you want to have in your life. It's really important to remember that you will ALWAYS have choices and you must never be afraid of making choices that feel right in your heart of hearts.

You are an AMAZING little person and I love you with all my heart, without conditions – I love you for who you are, for all the things you do. I am going to help you grow and make life what you want it to be. You deserve to live the life you choose. You deserve to live your best life, and I will make sure you can because I believe in you.

Right now I want you to lift up your head and feel really, really tall and proud of being you. Smile that beautiful smile. Smile so much that you can feel it on the inside AND the outside. That's beautiful. You are beautiful and I love you. You can - and deserve to – do everything you dream of. Go get 'em tiger!! You can do this!!"

3. TRACK YOUR QUALITIES

This exercise is good especially if you struggle to identify your own qualities, or even feel you have none at all.

If this is you, you may feel uncomfortable doing the exercise but please persevere as it will be worth it!

Exercise 3 - Track your Qualities

Ask someone you trust to help you compile a list of your qualities (do not edit this or argue with them!!).

Write them below (or in your notebook).

Use the tracker table to write down your qualities (in the 'Quality' column) then tick the 'Evidence' boxes each time you notice your qualities and pop the date in the box.

Here are examples of personal qualities to get you started in your conversation with your trusted friend/partner/family member. The list is NOT exhaustive but is just intended to give you some inspiration!

Example Personal Qualities:

- Good at ...(gardening, cooking, making things, sewing, drawing, DIY...)
- Kind
- Thoughtful
- Patient
- Caring
- Practical
- Helpful
- Funny
- Inspiring

- Sporty
- Tenacious
- Ambitious
- Hard-working
- Self-motivated
- Enthusiastic
- Conscientious
- Honest
- Humble
- Likeable
- Sincere
- Witty
- Quick-thinking
- Playful
- Open-minded
- Fair
- Loyal
- Reliable
- Flexible
- Positive
- Able to see the bigger picture
- Forgiving
- A natural leader
- Perceptive
- A team player
- Able to put people at ease

<u>My Notes</u>

Quality	Evidence (date)	Evidence (date)	Evidence (date)	Evidence (date)

4. YOUR QUALITIES = YOUR ASSETS

Remember that your personal qualities are YOUR assets, to use and share in the best possible way for the benefit of EVERYONE (and that includes YOU).

Just because you possess certain qualities, or skills, doesn't mean that you are obliged to use them 24/7. Nature did not intend everything to be happening continuously without respite - there are cycles and rest periods in everything, from farmers leaving a field to rest in order to keep land fertile, to animals who hibernate and conserve energy in winter. Our clever human brain gives us the ability to override the warning signs that we are tired and need to take a break from caring for people, working, answering the phone to a friend who's depressed, working out at the gym etc.

Women in particular often feel mean if they believe someone wants them to do something that they are able to do, but don't want to do. One of my clients, Sally, is very kind and caring, a good listener and excellent cook. Her grown-up son had moved back home after a relationship break-up and Sally did everything for him (cooking, cleaning, laundry) and even chauffeured him around if he went out with friends and wanted to have a few beers. Her friends and colleagues always phoned her if they wanted advice - Sally often answered calls late at night, even if she was already in bed. She knew she could help, and make everyone feel better and didn't feel able to say 'no'. She came to me completely burned out and even had to take time off work for exhaustion.

We're going to look at boundaries in the next chapter, but I'd like to share an exercise that helped Sally see that it was okay to say 'no': I'd like you to practise seeing your qualities as you see any other type of asset you may have, ie something that belongs to you but you don't constantly use, or use up in one go!

Imagine you have a total of £2000 in savings (your assets).

Over the course of a few weeks you receive requests in emails and letters for donations to charities that are close to your heart.

Will you give them everything in your savings account, leaving nothing at all for a rainy day?

I suspect you won't - you *may* give them <u>some</u> of your money, but will make sure you have enough for your needs.

It's the same with your qualities - just because you have them doesn't mean you have to use them until you are unable to give any more! If you do, you risk burning out completely, like Sally, and no-one at all will be able to benefit from your amazing qualities.

Just as your savings are there to help <u>you</u> and not just others, so are your qualities. It is **absolutely okay** to use your qualities for yourself!

Give yourself permission to use your qualities for your own benefit. So, if you are very good at caring for people and making them feel loved and nurtured for example, it's time to start practising some self-care. (We've got a whole chapter on self-care coming up if you need some inspiration!) If you usually spend your money on things for other people, I want you to treat yourself to something nice this week or this month. Whatever you do for others in fact, I'd like you to see how it feels to turn the tables and do it for you!

If you are finding it hard to give yourself permission, **I** am giving you permission to **be your own best friend**, and to <u>personally</u> enjoy your qualities.

REMEMBER - YOU ABSOLUTELY DESERVE TO RECEIVE 'GIFTS' (BENEFIT FROM YOUR ASSETS) AS MUCH AS <u>ANYONE</u> ELSE ON THIS PLANET!

Exercise 4 - Use your Gifts to Make your Life Better

Complete the following table to note down some of your qualities that you are going to use for YOUR own benefit!

Quality	How I can use it On myself
Eg looking after people	*Look after myself - I will make and use my own self-care bag*
Eg good at cooking	*I am going to cook MY favourite meal*

5. SET SOME BOUNDARIES

Having clear, healthy boundaries is essential for our general wellbeing and greatly affects our ability to function effectively. Boundaries enable us to feel in control and this feeling feeds into our self-confidence. Unfortunately, some of us don't feel we deserve to set limits or don't feel able to articulate them and so poor boundaries/low self-esteem become a vicious cycle.

I tackle the topic of boundaries in depth in another book and will try to just cover some key elements here and share an exercise that will help you on your way.

Many people are not aware they have boundary issues as they can often be disguised as other problems:

Relationship/interpersonal difficulties

Inability to say 'no'

Frequent feelings of anger, resentment or guilt

Struggling to get things done

Poor self-care

Let's drill down a bit and see why these problems occur if you have low self-confidence or low self-esteem.

Relationship/interpersonal difficulties
- Because you are afraid to speak up when you feel you are not being respected
- Because you never learned what it feels like to be respected

Inability to say 'no'
- Because you are afraid someone won't like you if you refuse to do something
- Because you want to please others and don't consider what it costs you

Frequent feelings of anger, resentment or guilt
- You may not express anger or resentment out loud, or you may not recognise that this is how you are feeling, but you may have a sense that everyone else gets what they need and nobody cares about you
- Feelings of guilt are frequent when you try to say 'no' but are not convinced it's okay (and so you end up reversing your answer and doing it anyway)

Struggling to get things done
- If you allow yourself to be pulled in all directions by others you may find it difficult to stay on task
- You could spend so much time helping other people that you don't have the energy to do your own stuff

Poor self-care
- It may feel like there's no time left for yourself by the time you've taken care of everyone else's needs
- Because you don't feel you deserve to be cared for

All boundaries start with YOU! If you are clear on the what, why and when you can set boundaries that sit well with you, that you are confident about, that you can communicate clearly, that won't leave you feeling guilty. So let's start by creating a little space for you to begin getting clear on YOUR needs and wants, and a reminder that your requirements are JUST as important as anyone else's (spot the recurring theme here!).

Exercise 5 - Why Not me?!

Grab your notepad, find a quiet, comfortable space and get yourself a warm drink or drink of water.

Think about the following areas of your life and write down one thing that you would like for yourself in each area:

Family

Friendships

Romantic Relationships

Health & Wellbeing

Work

Finances

Hobbies

Travel

Relaxation

Home

Pets

Food

Sleep

Spirituality

Possessions

Now, look at what you've written and ask yourself the following questions:

1. Are these wishes impossible to achieve? (Did you say, for example, that you want to fly to the moon tomorrow in a hot air balloon?)

2. Does anyone else in the world have the things you want?

If your answer to the first question is 'No, this is not impossible', and your answer to the second is 'Yes, others have these things' ask yourself a third question: 'So, why not me?'

You were born just as worthy of a fulfilling life as anyone else on this planet, so why don't you deserve the things on your list? Absolutely no reason at all!

Until you feel able to give yourself permission to have these things, I am giving you permission right here and now. Take a moment to let that sink in! This is your time!

Exercise 6 - Respect & Protect My Wishes

Complete the following table (and continue the list in your notebook if you need more space) by noting your wishes from Exercise 5 in the first column.

Next write some simple 'rules' for yourself that you will share with others as and when appropriate.

As always, start small and add to your rules as you go along.

Congratulations! You have started to put your boundaries in place!

My Wishes	How I will Respect & Protect my Wishes
Eg get more sleep	Put my phone on 'Do Not Disturb' from 10pm to 7am*
Eg have a weekend away	Block it on the calendar and let everyone know in advance

*Ask someone to help you with technical stuff if you don't know how! You can still allow calls from certain callers in case of real emergencies but think carefully about who really needs to go on that list.

6. FREE YOURSELF FROM THE PAST

Sometimes we are aware of who or what left us feeling worthless in the past but it isn't always so clear cut. These exercises will help you identify and free yourself from beliefs that have kept you small until now.

As I've said before, please seek professional help if you have experienced serious abuse or trauma of any kind and don't try these exercises until you have therapeutic support in place.

Exercise 7 - Identify past Hurts that affected your Self-Confidence

If you need to, give yourself a few minutes with your eyes closed and remember some recent times when you were aware of not feeling confident or worthy. Think about one at a time and imagine each example as a weed poking up from the earth, with long roots reaching deep into the soil. If you could follow those roots to find similar examples from your earlier life what would you discover?

Take your time and just see what comes up for you. Make notes about what happened plus who was involved, how old you were, where you were.

Remember to give yourself a break if you find this hard to do.

Exercise 8 - Free Yourself from past hurts that affected your self-confidence

1. On the following page write down the names of people from the previous exercise who have undermined your self confidence in your past. This may have been when you were a child **or** during your adult years.

Don't worry if you're not sure you can remember everyone and everything as you can repeat this exercise as many times as you like.

2. When you've finished writing your notes use the following script to help you let go. (You are welcome to use your own words - just make sure you cover each part.)

"[Name(s)], I now know that whatever you did or said to me was actually about YOU - your own insecurities, fears, past experiences, or beliefs.
I will leave these things with you. You must make your peace with them.

[Name(s)], I am ready to forgive you and to let go of these hurts so they may heal. I now know that I have so many reasons to feel good about myself.

[Name(s)], I now understand that I am perfectly me. I see that I can make my own choices now, and I am choosing to turn my back on the past so that I can look to the future."

Now you can choose what to do with your notes - burn them, rip them up, drop them into the sea or a river...

Repeat this exercise as many times as you need.

People who have hurt me and/or undermined my self-confidence:

Name	What they did or said...

Name	What they did or said...

7. SET YOURSELF A CHALLENGE

It's important to measure how you are growing your confidence so set yourself regular challenges! The challenges should be small at first so you can gradually build up to bigger ones.

Research has shown that when we set ourselves goals we are more successful if we write them down, so keep notes that you can look back over.

You can keep your notes private if you prefer, but it may also be helpful to share your challenges with a supportive, non-judgemental friend.

Exercise 9 - Choose your Challenge

1. Choose a challenge for yourself (eg write a letter of complaint/be more confident on next girls' night out)
2. Define your goal clearly so you can measure it (eg I will write a letter of complaint and be clear in what I want to happen/ walk confidently into the room with my head high and shoulders down and will ask each person in my group at least one question)
3. Decide what small actions you will take to prepare for this (eg write a list of bullet points and decide what outcome I want *or* choose outfit I love, practise walking round bedroom confidently in outfit, write out some questions I can ask people)

GOOD LUCK - AND ENJOY YOUR MISSIONS!

8. HOT POTATOES

I often use my 'hot potato' analogy when talking to clients with low self-esteem who believe if someone is in a bad mood it's because of something **they** have done.

People with low self-confidence often allow others to project their moods, opinions, thoughts and actions onto them and assume that the other person is upset with them.

I firstly remind my clients that anything that is done or said (or implied) by another person is a reflection of their own fears, worries, experiences etc. inside their own mind.

Secondly I invite clients to imagine that everybody's fears and experiences are like hot potatoes!

We all need to do something with these spuds because they're burning our hands and are stopping us from reaching out for the nice things in life, but many people simply try to make others hold them so they don't have to deal with them.

If you are someone who doesn't care about your hands being burnt (you don't think you're worth looking after) you are leaving yourself wide open to receiving loads of hot spuds that you actually have no business holding.

LEAVE OTHERS TO DEAL WITH THEIR OWN HOT POTATOES!

Trust that they will work out what to do in their situations and leave them to it! Trust that the universe will help them figure it out because it really is **not** your job.

Of course, we're talking about able-minded adults here, not children or other genuine dependents!

Exercise 10 - Leave it with Them

1. Over the next day I'd like you to just notice who in your life tries to throw their hot potatoes your way. Be an observer and notice your reactions without judgement. Make a few notes in your book.
2. The following day you're going to 'catch' at least one of these moments when you notice someone's words or actions triggers a sense of guilt or responsibility and practise saying in your head "I'm going to leave that with you. You need to sort that out. It's not my job."
3. Over time you'll be able to build up opportunities to put this into practice and I'd like you to celebrate each time you refuse to take on someone else's hot potatoes!

It may also help to create a shield of some sort for yourself, and visualise this shield each time someone else is behaving in a way that triggered you in the past.

Picturing a protective bubble, a force field, or a ring of guardians around you that will deflect those spuds works for a lot of people. Why not give it a try?

9. DEALING WITH 'WHAT IF'S'

As we've said before, having a sense of control can help us feel more confident. One of the ways we can make this happen is by using our negative thoughts and fears to create contingency plans.

Read on to find out how!

Exercise 11

1. Note down a few things you have recently worried about - or are currently worried about - using 'What if...?' sentences.

Examples
A **What if** I'm late for the meeting?
B **What if** our flight is delayed?
C **What if** I find a lump in my breast?

2. Now write a *positive* version of each sentence and sit with those thoughts for a few minutes. These scenarios are just as likely to happen - more so in most cases!

Examples
A **What if** I arrive early for the meeting? (I'll have time to stretch my legs and read through my notes.)
B **What if** our flight isn't delayed? (We'll arrive in plenty of time for our transfers.)
C **What if** I don't find a lump in my breast? (I can just carry on making the most out of each day.)

3. Prepare your contingency plan for each event you wrote about in 1. Using '**If...then...**'

Examples
A **What if** I'm late for the meeting?
If I'm late for the meeting **then** I'll call or text the organiser to apologise, give my ETA and I'll ask to chat to them after the meeting.
B **What if** our flight is delayed?
If our flight is delayed **then** we'll contact the transfer company to reschedule and will have extra time to browse the duty-free shops or read a magazine/have a coffee.
C **What if** I find a lump in my breast?
If I find a lump in my breast **then** I'll get it checked out as soon as possible so I can get early treatment and fully recover if it's cancer.

4. Now you can park those 'What if' worries because you have a plan should the worst happen, and get on with your life!

10. TIME TO LOOK AFTER YOU

As I've said before, you deserve to be taken care of as much as anyone else. Even if you haven't really looked after yourself or felt worthy of self-care in the past, you can start by taking small actions TODAY. Because you ARE worth it!

If you set up the following two self-care strategies it will be so easy to just dip in for short bursts of time. The more you practise the more you will start to believe in your worthiness. Over time your self-confidence will most definitely grow.

Exercise 12 - My Wellbeing Toolkit

Make a list of things that have made you feel calmer or improved your mental wellbeing in the past, or things you believe may be helpful. Include a variety of ideas that take different lengths of time to use at home and at work.
You could write these out on a sheet of nice paper or design the list on your computer or phone (canva.com has some fabulous free design tools you can use).
Make a few copies and keep your toolkit list in different places so you've always got one to hand.

Here are some ideas to get you started:

- Listen to relaxing music
- Go for a walk
- Phone a friend
- Sing
- Yoga

- Have your favourite meal
- Book in with a coach or therapist
- Write down how you're feeling
- Watch something funny
- Physical exercise
- Have an early night
- Wash your hair/shave and get dressed
- Have a massage
- Read or listen to a self- help book
- Jogging
- Treat yourself to a little gift (anything from a new magazine to a new gadget!)
- Have a bath
- Call a helpline
- Make a list of 10 things you are grateful for
- Change the layout of your desk/office/bedroom
- Do a random or anonymous act of kindness
- List all of your achievements

Exercise 13 - Create a Self-Care Pack for yourself

Make a list of around 10 items you can put in a bag or a box for yourself to dip into on days you're feeling down or are struggling with something (see below for suggestions).

Start collecting the things TODAY and keep topping up your supplies so you always have an abundance of things to chose from.

You can also just dip into your pack on a daily basis - set aside 10 minutes when you get in from work, for example, before walking the dog or fixing the evening meal.

- fluffy socks
- compilation of feel-good music
- scented candle
- photos of good times
- funny book
- sachet of luxury hot chocolate
- bubble bath
- face masks
- DVD
- essential oil
- Scrap book or mood board to add pictures & ideas of future plans
- book of short stories
- collection of meaningful, inspirational quotes
- voucher to spend online
- magazine
- puzzle book
- colouring book & colour pencils
- favourite movie playlist
- other luxury toiletries/beauty products

WRAPPING THINGS UP!

Thank you so much for reading my book! I hope you've enjoyed it and found stuff that resonated with you! If you did like it, it would mean so much if you could leave a review on Amazon for me to help spread the word.

Before we leave each other I would like you to take 2 minutes to choose 1 action, however small, that you are going to take TODAY and make a promise to yourself right now.

I   [your name]

commit to taking action today that will help to boost my self-confidence.

I will do [write exercise number or other action here]

Signed

Date

Congratulations! You have taken that all-important first step.

Go at your own pace, building up healthy practices that work for YOU.

Please share your self-confidence wins by tagging me in social media @notjustcoaching (Instagram) or @hypnocoachingGB (Twitter & Facebook).

I can't wait to hear how your new chapter is going!

YOU HAVE GOT THIS!

YOU DESERVE THIS!

My Very Best Wishes

Amanda x

ABOUT THE AUTHOR

Amanda Craven is one of the UK's top 5* reviewed Clinical Hypnotherapists and Life Coaches. She is passionate about her work and the transformations it brings about.

To date she has helped over a thousand clients live their best life through her unique approach to overcoming anxiety, trauma, low self-esteem and setting life goals.

Amanda regularly shares free life coaching tips and ideas on her YouTube channel: youtube.com/c/notjustcoaching

To join her free email community and receive weekly life-coaching tips and exclusive offers go to

resources.amandacraven.org/newsletter-signup

For more information on ways to work with Amanda take a look at

amandacraven.org

Printed in Great Britain
by Amazon

80804111R00037